DATE DUE			

READ ABOUT THE
POLICEMAN

READ ABOUT THE
POLICEMAN

written and illustrated by

Louis Slobodkin

FRANKLIN WATTS, INC.
575 Lexington Avenue
New York, N.Y. 10022

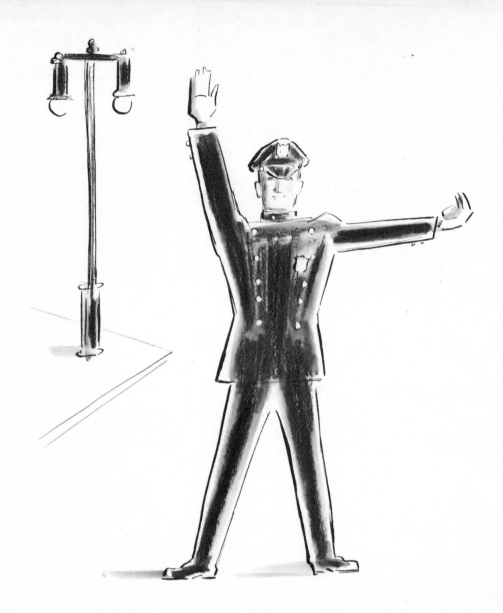

SBN 531-01263-8

Library of Congress Catalog Card Number: 66-10582

Printed in the United States of America

4 5

If anyone thinks that all he has to do to become a policeman is to grow up big and strong, he is wrong. That may have been true years ago, but it is not true now!

Five hundred years ago, there were no policemen. Very rich people hired big, strong men who were good fighters with swords and clubs to protect them and their treasures from robbers and other troublemakers.

5

8143

The poorer people could not afford to hire strong men to protect them. They usually buried their few treasures in a secret place, and hoped that the robbers would not find the hiding place. If robbers came to steal a poor man's sheep or cattle, he and his sturdy sons (if he had any sturdy sons) tried to fight the robbers off.

Later on, in towns and cities, the people each gave a little money, and together they hired men to protect them all. Those men were called watchmen. They were perhaps the first policemen. Of course, they were not policemen as we know them now.

A watchman did not wear a uniform. He had no training as a policeman. All he did was march around the town at night with a lantern and a heavy staff.

Every hour he called out, "One o'clock and all is well," or "Two o'clock and all is well," and so on, all through the night.

The townspeople awakened by the watchman's shout would go back to sleep knowing they were safe until the watchman came back again at the next hour and shouted, "All is well."

If a watchman saw any thieves or robbers at their dishonest work he aroused the neighborhood and called the other watchmen with his shouts, and beat the thieves or robbers with his heavy staff.

In some towns that had no money to pay the watchmen, the men of the town volunteered and took their turns working as watchmen.

Over three hundred years ago, when New York City was governed by the Dutch and was called New Amsterdam, there were no police, of course. When the Dutch first came to what is now called Manhattan Island, New York City, they should have had some policemen. It is said that a tribe of

Canarsie Indians, who really lived in what is now called Brooklyn on Long Island, sold Manhattan to the Dutchmen for twenty-four dollars' worth of trinkets.

Then the Canarsie Indians loaded their trinkets into their canoes and paddled back to Brooklyn. The Dutchmen had to pay the real owners, the Manhattan Indians, for Manhattan Island.

A good police force would have protected the Dutchmen from the Canarsie swindlers.

Not long after the Dutchmen settled in New Amsterdam, they hired eight watchmen to police the town. The watchmen carried large wooden rattles, or whirligigs, and were called the "rattle watch" (or "Rattel-Wacht," as the Dutch said).

When the rattle watchmen saw a robber breaking into a house or when they saw someone else committing a crime they chased the criminal, whirling their big noisy wooden rattles. The noise of the wooden rattles did two things. It scared the criminals, and it called other watchmen and woke up the townspeople to come and help catch the criminals.

Nowadays, policemen carry a whistle that they blow to call other policemen.

Sometime later, after the British captured New Amsterdam and renamed the city New York, the first uniformed policemen appeared in America. That was about 1694. The Mayor of New York ordered the watchmen all to wear the same kind of colored clothes and a sort of badge, which was the coat of arms of New York. This badge was sewed on their coats.

These men were drilled, and trained to shoot a musket — that is, an old-fashioned shoulder gun. They were not trained the way our policemen are today, though.

During the next one hundred years, from 1700 to 1800, the City of New York grew larger, and so did the police force. In 1700, there were just twelve watchmen or policemen, and in about 1844 there were over one thousand.

By this time, many things had come about. All New York policemen wore hard leather hats to protect their heads from stones and clubs of the unfriendly people who attacked them. They were nicknamed "leatherheads." The policemen carried clubs 33 inches long, to defend themselves and to control the robbers and other wrongdoers.

Around 1828, in London, England, a man named Sir Robert Peel set up the first modern city police force. The London policemen were called, and are

still called, "Bobbies" because of Sir Robert. The New York police and the police of many other cities all over the world used some of Sir Robert Peel's ideas in setting up their own police forces.

Then, for the first time, policemen began to wear metal badges. The New York police wore eight-pointed stars made of copper, and some people say that's how the old nickname "cop" came about. "Cop" is short for copper, they say.

Now policemen were really beginning to get a little training for their jobs. Before this, policemen and watchmen were chosen only because they were big and strong and were able to use a club or a gun or a sword.

For example, in London, England, about 1800, a champion prizefighter named Daniel Mendoza was chosen to be a sheriff's officer, a sort of policeman, only because he was a good strong fighter.

Daniel Mendoza also had a kind heart. He stopped being a sheriff's officer and went back to prizefighting because he could not bear to arrest old widow ladies for not paying their debts. In those days, people who did not pay their debts were arrested and thrown into prison, even if they owed someone only a few cents.

It so happened that Daniel Mendoza, who became the champion prizefighter of Ireland, was not only strong and kind. He was able to write a few books, too, so he must have had some education. Most of the policemen, though, were picked only because they were strong or because they could handle clubs and guns and other weapons.

A number of years later — about 1865 — there were no regular policemen in America's great Wild West. Brave cowboys who were good shots were hired to protect people and their cattle and their money from the outlaws and the savage Indians.

Some of those brave cowboys had been slaves and were freed after the Civil War.

One of the bravest of those cowboys who had been a slave was Bose Ikard. He worked for Charles Goodnight, one of the most famous cattlemen in Texas. Many a time Charles Goodnight and Bose Ikard fought outlaws and Comanche Indians

together. When Bose Ikard died peacefully of old age, Charles Goodnight had a gravestone put up for his friend. On it were these words:

Bose Ikard
Served with me four years on the Goodnight-Loving Trail. He never shirked on duty or disobeyed an order. He rode with me in many stampedes — participated in three engagements with Comanches, splendid behavior.

Charles Goodnight

Another cowboy who had been a slave was named George Washington. He was a friend of the great outlaw, Billy the Kid. The Governor of New Mexico

sent George Washington out to find and bring back Billy the Kid. And that's what he did.

In the West there were also regular sheriffs and marshals who fought the outlaws, cattle rustlers, and wild Indians. Sometimes when a sheriff had to chase a gang of outlaws he picked cowboys who were fast with their guns to go along with him in his posse.

Of course, none of those cowboys or sheriffs had much training or education as policemen. They were just brave, strong men who could ride fast and shoot fast.

Now that police forces were being set up in all the big cities and towns, policemen all over the world were being trained for their jobs. This all happened between 1835 and 1850. The first detectives began to appear. Policemen were being taught to know about the laws of the land. They learned other things to do besides just chasing robbers.

They began to watch for parents who did not take proper care of their children. They looked for lawbreakers who drove their horses through the city streets at a speed of over five miles an hour.

The detectives received undercover training.

That is, they studied how to find criminals after the crimes had been done, and they learned how to follow and track down criminals. They were nicknamed "shadows."

In 1858, New York City began to pick more carefully the men who would be trained to be policemen. These men had to be able to read and write English, and they had to be at least five feet eight inches tall. They could not start to be policemen if they were over thirty-five years old. These men must not have a criminal record. That means that they must never have been arrested for committing a crime.

During the following years the New York Police Force grew bigger and better. That was true of the police forces of all the cities of the United States and the rest of the world, too.

The Mounted Squad, the policemen on horse-back, appeared in New York around 1871. It was at about that time that one of the duties of the New York policemen was to clean the city streets. Ten years later, after the Street Cleaning Department was formed, this duty was taken away from the Police Department.

A little later, the Detective Bureau was created. Soon after, in 1888, the first policewomen were appointed to the Police Force. Then came the Police Bicycle Squad.

Police departments of all the great cities of the world studied the police systems in other cities. In Paris, France, the police worked out a way of keeping records of known criminals. It was called the Bertillon system. The policemen measured the criminals' heads, and they measured their fingers and their left foot, and so on. They kept all these measurements on a card along with a photograph of each criminal.

In that way they thought they could recognize any criminal, no matter how he disguised himself. The New York police and the London police used that system from Paris for a while, but they gave it up for the fingerprint system.

A long time ago, in Asia, it was discovered that each person's fingerprints are different from any other person's fingerprints — and fingerprints never change.

In ancient times, Asiatic kings pressed their thumbprints down on all important papers such as new laws or orders, instead of signing their names.

Around 1900, the police of Bengal, India, had begun taking fingerprints of criminals and keeping a record of them.

If a burglar or a robber came into a house and touched anything — a glass or some shiny surface — the police would find the robber's fingerprints. Then they would compare those fingerprints with all the fingerprints of known burglars and robbers that they had collected. At last, when they found the proper burglar or robber, they searched for him and arrested him.

The fingerprint system is still considered one of the best ways of finding a criminal after he has committed a crime.

But taking fingerprints is only one of the scientific ways of finding people who are guilty of crime. The police of London and New York and the other great cities have discovered many scientific methods and they have learned from each other.

23

In the meanwhile, the big police forces of the
great cities kept on growing. Today there are over
twenty-eight thousand policemen in New York.

Here is what a modern New York policeman is
really like. Policemen in other big cities are much
the same.

First of all, the men who are trained to become
policemen are young men — men in their twen-
ties. Many of them have already served in the
United States Army or Navy.

To begin with, a man who wants to be a policeman in New York must be a United States citizen
between the ages of twenty and twenty-nine. He
must be a graduate of elementary school and high
school. (Many of the policemen have gone to col-

lege, too.) He must be at least five feet eight inches tall, with good eyesight and good hearing.

Then he must pass a written examination with high marks, to show how smart he is and how quickly he can think. He must pass a medical examination to show that he is healthy and strong and can move quickly, too. He must prove he has a good character and that he has not committed any crimes or been in trouble of any kind.

He must have a license to drive an automobile, and he must live in or very near New York City.

He begins his training as a policeman only after he has passed all these tests and examinations. Young women must pass much the same tests if they wish to be policewomen.

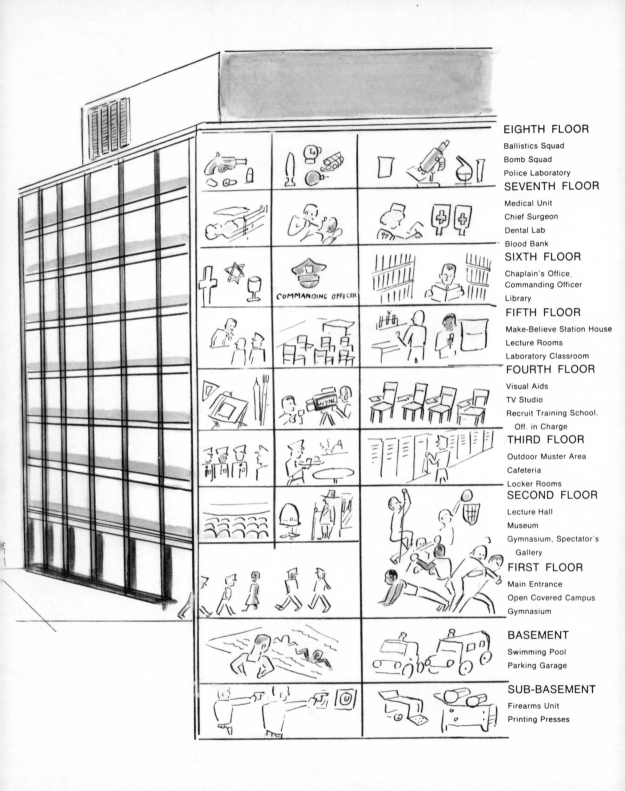

EIGHTH FLOOR

Ballistics Squad
Bomb Squad
Police Laboratory

SEVENTH FLOOR

Medical Unit
Chief Surgeon
Dental Lab
Blood Bank

SIXTH FLOOR

Chaplain's Office,
Commanding Officer
Library

FIFTH FLOOR

Make-Believe Station House
Lecture Rooms
Laboratory Classroom

FOURTH FLOOR

Visual Aids
TV Studio
Recruit Training School,
Off. in Charge

THIRD FLOOR

Outdoor Muster Area
Cafeteria
Locker Rooms

SECOND FLOOR

Lecture Hall
Museum
Gymnasium, Spectator's
Gallery

FIRST FLOOR

Main Entrance
Open Covered Campus
Gymnasium

BASEMENT

Swimming Pool
Parking Garage

SUB-BASEMENT

Firearms Unit
Printing Presses

There is a beautiful big building on East 20th Street in New York City. It is the Police Academy. That is the place where a New York policeman trains. He goes to this school, or academy, for four months. Here he studies all sorts of things that a modern policeman must know. Not only does he learn the best way to catch criminals, but he learns how to protect people and how to save lives.

First aid, how to swim to save lives, wrestling, judo, and shooting are among the many things he learns at the academy.

A policeman must be trained so that he can race along dark streets, jump over backyard fences — when he is chasing robbers or other lawbreakers

— rush up flights of stairs, carry sick or injured people, shinny up bridge cables or dive into icy waters to save people, and do many other things that will be a part of his job.

He is trained to be good at these things so that he can help and protect other people, and also protect or save his own life if he is attacked by robbers, murderers, or other nasty wrongdoers while he is carrying out his duty.

The young policeman, who is now called a "recruit" policeman or nicknamed a "rookie" police-

man, studies what his many duties are. He studies the criminal laws of the city, and other laws that have to do with his work.

All through the four months that he is studying, the young recruit policeman is paid, just as a regular policeman is. The rookie is not paid as much, but almost as much.

The Police Academy has a big library full of books about police work and the laws. It has a big laboratory full of the latest scientific instruments used to detect crime. There is a wonderful big gym-

nasium, an immense swimming pool, and a very modern shooting gallery.

There are fine big classrooms and a marvelous museum full of old and new police history. Any boy or girl who lives in or visits New York ought to visit the Police Academy and the Museum someday. The policemen there are very polite and are glad to show anyone around the place.

When the young recruit policeman is through at the Academy he gets some more training in a police station house, and at last he becomes a regular policeman. But he does not stop studying how to be a better policeman.

Of course, when people see a policeman walking along the street watching out that there is no trouble, or standing out in the road directing traffic, or riding around in a patrol car, these people cannot be expected to know all the good things that policemen do.

Here is part of a long list of police duties.

Policemen find lost children. If a child is lost he should look for a policeman and tell the policeman his name and address. The policeman will see that he is taken home safely.

Policemen help people who become sick on the street or have accidents.

Policemen stop people who are cruel to little children or animals.

They stop people who drive dangerously fast along the city streets.

They watch out for all the things that will be dangerous to people or may hurt them.

If anyone sees something that may be dangerous — like an open sewer, or something that may
topple off a roof — he should tell a policeman at
once. The policeman will see to it that the danger
is removed.

Late at night, after people have locked up their
stores, a policeman goes around and tries the doors
of the stores, to be really sure that they are locked.

When great crowds gather, the policeman tells
people which way to go or where to stand so that

they will not hurt each other accidentally.

Policemen tell people how to get to different places in the city.

A policeman does so many things to help and protect the people of the city that a complete list of his duties and everything he does would fill a number of books.

Even though a policeman works eight hours a day, when he goes off duty he must carry with him at all times his badge, or his shield, and his regulation revolver. Even when he is not wearing his uniform, he must be prepared to take proper police action whenever he sees a crime committed or notices some other trouble.

A policeman is never really off duty.

Among the twenty-eight thousand members of the New York Police Department, over eighteen thousand of them are regular precinct patrolmen. A "precinct" is a district of a city. A "patrolman" is a policeman who has his headquarters at a precinct station house, and patrols, or guards and watches, certain streets or places in his district. The over eighteen thousand New York patrolmen work out of eighty police stations that are placed all over the city.

The commanding officer of the whole city Police Force and all the station houses is the Chief Inspector. Of course, he has many assistants.

At the head of each station house is a police captain. In the station house there are four lieutenants and nine police sergeants. They all have very important duties. They tell the patrolmen where they are needed when calls for help come in. They make out reports about the people patrolmen arrest and bring to the station house, and they do many other things.

The captain or another officer in the station house tells the patrolman that he must walk along certain streets and watch and guard them or other places not too far from the station house.

On a certain street there may be some very important banks or stores that need to be protected from robbers. Then the patrolman may guard only a few blocks of this street.

Or he may patrol a number of long blocks, if they are on peaceful streets where there usually is not much trouble. For eight hours he walks back and forth along the streets that are called his "post," or "beat." He watches for any disturbance there. If anything unusual happens, he takes care of it. When the eight hours are up, another patrolman comes along and takes his place, and the first

patrolman checks out at the station house and then goes home.

A third patrolman takes the place of the second patrolman after another eight hours have passed. So, for twenty-four hours through every day and night, patrolmen watch all over the city. They try to stop trouble and they try to protect people and property.

Police signal boxes with telephones in them are placed along the street. These are used by the patrolman. He calls his station house every hour to get new orders if there are any. Or he just tells the officers at the station house that he is all right and is doing his duty and they will not have to worry about him.

If a patrolman does not telephone his station house when he should, a patrol car is sent out at once to find out what is the matter.

The police signal boxes may be used by ordinary people too, if they have to call a policeman. (But *don't ever* call the police unless you really need them. They are too busy to waste time answering false alarms.)

Radio patrol cars work with regular patrolmen. There are about five hundred patrol cars in the New York Police Department. Each car carries two policemen and has a two-way radio. Suppose there is trouble somewhere, and someone calls for the police on the telephone. Within two minutes, at least one patrol car, and sometimes more, will come racing to answer that call for help.

A regular patrolman also calls for patrol cars if he needs help.

There are many divisions and special squads in the New York Police Department. One of the most important is the Detective Division.

The Detective Division

The 3,500 policemen and policewomen who are picked for the Detective Division are chosen because they are especially good at certain things. They get special training too.

Almost every regular patrolman would like someday to become a detective. If he shows that he can do some special things and he knows how to investigate crimes, he may be appointed to the Detective Division.

The head of the detectives is the Chief of Detectives. There are many squads that make up the whole Detective Division. Here are some of them.

The Homicide Squad

These are the detectives who try to find and arrest the terrible person who has killed another person. They also investigate accidents where someone has been killed.

The Burglary Squad

The detectives of this squad track down gangs of burglars. Sometimes they spend months in disguise as they follow known burglars who plan to rob a house or a bank. Of course, they must catch the burglars at work or with the goods they have stolen, or they cannot arrest them.

The Auto Squad

These detectives go after thieves who steal cars or parts of cars.

The Forgery Squad

Their job is to track down and arrest criminals called forgers, who write checks and sign someone else's name to them. The men in this squad also look for forgers who use and write down the names of other people in order to steal money, jewels, or other property.

BANK

The Missing Persons Unit

These detectives search for people who have disappeared from their homes and families. They look in the hospitals to see if a missing person had an accident, and they look in many other places. They use all sorts of things in searching for a missing person. They telephone and send letters and telegrams all over the country. They put photographs of the missing person on television and in the newspapers. They use the best scientific methods to find the missing person.

The Bomb Squad

This is one of the bravest squads of detectives. (All detectives and policemen are very brave men, but I, the author of this book, think these detectives are among the bravest.) Since 1903 the men of the Bomb Squad in the New York Police Department have been risking their lives to save other people from getting hurt or killed.

This is what they do.

When some foolish or very mean person makes a dangerous bomb and hides it somewhere, the Bomb Squad goes to work. They hunt for the bomb

while they know that it may go off at any second
— even before they find it. When they do find the
bomb, they *very, very* carefully try to fix it at once
so that it will not go off. If they cannot do that, one
or two detectives *very, very* carefully pick up the
bomb and carry it to a special truck, and they carefully drive away.

Then, when they get the bomb in a safe place
away from other people, they take it apart so that
it cannot go off.

Of course, the detectives in this squad take every
possible precaution. They are *very, very* careful,
and they have the most modern scientific methods
for handling bombs. Even so, their work is still ter-
ribly dangerous.

The Ballistics Squad

The ballistics detectives are specialists in guns and bullets. Whenever a person is hurt or killed by a gun, or whenever a gun is used to commit a crime, the Ballistics Squad is called in by the other policemen or detectives to help.

Sometimes the ballistics detectives find discharged shells or bullets near the place where the crime was committed. The detectives can tell very quickly what kind of gun was used in the crime, and they can tell many other facts. With their many wonderful scientific systems they help all members of the Police Department.

The Safe, Loft and Truck Squad

These detectives are well trained in the ways of safe robbers, and they can often recognize criminals who are planning to rob a factory, a big warehouse, or a fancy hotel.

The Pickpocket Squad

Men and women detectives of this squad watch out in stores, theaters, or parks, or wherever crowds gather. The detectives try to catch sneak thieves who steal things out of people's pockets.

The Bureau of Criminal Investigations

Whenever a person commits a felony — a serious crime like murder or robbery — and the police catch him, he is arrested. Other people who behave badly by breaking certain important laws are also arrested. Each such person is photographed and his fingerprints are taken. Then everything that helps describe him is written down on cards — the color of his eyes and hair, any unusual scars he has, how tall he is, and much else. These cards are put away in the Bureau of Criminal Investigation.

When another crime is committed sometime later, fingerprints may be discovered near the

crime, or someone may be found who has seen the criminal at work. Then the B.C.I., the Bureau of Criminal Investigation, helps the detectives working on the case.

The fingerprints that the detectives found are compared with those in the B.C.I.'s collection of fingerprints. There may be some that match. The person who saw the criminal at work looks through the B.C.I.'s collection of photographs of known criminals. He picks one or two photographs that look like the criminal he saw. Now the detectives know whom to look for.

Sometimes the person who saw the criminal cannot find a photograph that seems familiar, even after he has looked through the B.C.I.'s collection. In that case, he describes the man he saw to police artists, and they draw the face of the criminal from what he tells them.

Many robberies and murders and other terrible crimes have been solved in this way, with the help of the B.C.I.

The Central Investigation Bureau

Sometimes a bright policeman or policewoman with a very good memory accidentally finds a clue to an old unsolved crime. The clue the police found is passed on to the Central Investigation Bureau (C.I.B.). If it is a good clue, the C.I.B. tells the different departments of the police force. They all go to work on the new clue and try to solve the old crime and capture the criminal or criminals.

The policeman with the good memory often gets promoted because he is bright. He may be promoted and become a regular detective. This can happen to a policewoman, too.

The men of the C.I.B. know about gangs of robbers and other criminals and they tell other departments of the police about them. The C.I.B. trades the information it has collected about criminals with all the police forces in the United States.

Besides those in the Detective Division, there are many other squads who do special work in the New York Police Department.

There is one called the Safety Division. These policemen — over 1,900 of them — do the main work of directing traffic and protecting the ten million people who move around New York as they go to school and as they go to work in the morning.

And again the police are there when the people go home from work or home from school. They are there betweentimes, too.

There is the Accident Investigation Squad. These policemen investigate the reason for accidents and find out whose fault it was when automobiles bump together or knock someone down, or when some other accident occurs.

There is the Steamship Squad. More than a million people come and go in the big steamships that sail in and out of New York Harbor. The policemen of the Steamship Squad give special attention to those travelers.

50

There are the famous Mounted Patrol — two
hundred and fifty of them, all riding beautiful
brown horses.

No one who has ever seen these fine-looking policemen riding their beautiful prancing horses at
the head of a parade on a New York street will soon
forget them.

But the Mounted Policemen do more than just
lead parades along the New York streets. They do
many important things. Whenever great crowds
gather in the city streets or in the city parks, the
Mounted Police help control and protect the people
so that they will not hurt themselves or each other.

The police horses are trained to work as a team with the policemen who ride on their backs. They are intelligent, good horses, and are very well taken care of. When they grow old — about fifteen or twenty years old — they are retired and placed in good homes where there are pleasant fields for them, and a good barn.

There are the Motorcycle Policemen with their white crash helmets. These policemen watch the roads and bridges around New York City to be sure no one races his car so fast that he will hurt himself or other people.

These motorcycle police are used sometimes to speed some necessary medicine to a very sick person or to someone who was hurt badly in an accident. They are helpful in protecting important visiting people as they ride about the city in their automobiles.

There are ten Emergency Service Squads that are placed in different parts of the city. These policemen are specially trained to care for people and animals who have met with an accident or fallen into a trap. There are thousands of people who are alive today because of the fine work of the Emergency Service Squads.

Each emergency squad has a special truck that contains over two hundred tools that can help people in trouble. There are all sorts of things for persons who have been gassed or who need artificial respiration. The squads have saved many people in

gas-filled or smoke-filled rooms. They have captured venomous snakes, and wild animals who have escaped. They have also rescued kittens who were stuck in drainpipes or were stranded high up in trees.

In their trucks the squads also carry rifles, machine guns, and tear gas, in case they have to use them to control desperate criminals. The squads have tools for dealing with the many kinds of accidents that can happen to people. There are tools that can jack up a subway train, and there are tools that can snip a child's ring off his finger if that ring is dangerous.

The Emergency Service Squads also have twenty-six two-man radio cars so that police can rush quickly to investigate a crime that is going on. The cars are used for other emergencies, too.

The Harbor Police Squad is one of the oldest in the Police Department. It was started in 1858. In those days, twelve policemen in rowboats used to row out into the harbor or into the rivers around

New York to try to catch the river pirates who preyed on the waterfront.

Now the Harbor Police have thirteen good strong ships, or launches. These launches are all named after policemen who died as heroes doing their duty.

The largest of the launches is 60 feet long, and the smallest is 15 feet long. They are sturdy ships that are used for special jobs. One has a bow built for breaking ice. Another is so flat-bottomed that it can be used to rescue people who get into the low marsh waters.

The Harbor Police help fight fire on the piers and in the warehouses along the waterfront. They have rescued people who have fallen into the harbor, and other people whose planes have crashed into the water. They have also grabbed escaping prisoners out of the water. (There are some prisons on the islands near New York.)

The Harbor Police have lassoed and pulled cows out of New York Harbor and have done many other useful things.

Each Harbor Police launch has two-way radios, equipment for fighting fires, searchlights, and all the things that the men need to do their work.

The Aviation Bureau of the New York Police Department was started in 1927. At first the policemen had only a three-seated amphibian. (That is an aeroplane that can take off from and land on either land or water.) But that old plane could really only carry two policemen. The third seat was always empty. The policemen who flew in that plane said that the angel who protected them sat in the third seat. That seat was called the "angel seat."

The air policemen made their first rescue when they saw two swimmers in the harbor being carried out to sea. The water was too rough for the plane to land, so one policeman jumped into the water from the plane and towed both swimmers to shore.

In 1947, the Police Department got its first helicopter. Now there are five helicopters. Four of them patrol New York and New York Harbor, and the fifth is used for training. The police helicopters have rescued many people. One of them rescued a steeplejack who was working on the top of St. John's Cathedral, one of the tallest churches in New York.

Another time, a police helicopter followed a homing pigeon to a house in Jamaica, Long Island, after a kidnapper had sent the pigeon to the father of a child who had been kidnapped. A ransom note was tied to the bird's leg.

The police helicopter followed that pigeon home again and captured the kidnapper and found the child.

8143

For seventy-five years the Bureau of Police Women has been an important part of the New York Police Department.

Policewomen have full police powers. They carry revolvers and handcuffs and make arrests just as policemen do. But they specialize in arresting such criminals as pickpockets, and shoplifters — the people who steal things from store counters — and unpleasant people who annoy women and children.

The policewomen guard and attend women who are arrested. They are especially good with lost children. Of course, policewomen are also most useful in all crimes that have to do with women and children who misbehave. There are 340 policewomen in the New York Police Force. About 65 of them are in the Detective Division.

The Youth Division of the Police Department is interested in young people and children. The patrolmen and policewomen in this division watch out for children and young people and try to help them and keep them from getting into trouble and making mistakes that they will be sorry for as long as they live.

The men and women in the Youth Division try to help children who have been badly treated by their parents or by other grown-ups. There are such parents — very few of them, but there are some.

The police in the Youth Division try to find children who have foolishly run away from home. Some of these children live in New York, and others live in distant places and come to New York.

Many of the members of this division are men and women who have been graduated from college and have studied the things that trouble children and make them behave the way they do.

The Police Athletic League, nicknamed P.A.L., is not a regular official part of the New York Police Department, but it works closely with the department.

P.A.L. is set up for the children of the city, to help them and to give them some fun so that they

won't get into trouble and break laws. There are forty-four play streets and playgrounds, thirty-five Youth Centers, and three Play Mobiles for the use of children.

The policemen and policewomen work for P.A.L. This is extra work that they do for the children of New York. It is true that all policemen and policewomen do many other things for the children because many of them are fathers and mothers of children and because they are a fine group of men and women who like children.

Not all the different squads and divisions of the New York Police Department are mentioned in this book. There would not be room enough to write about them all. If anyone wants to know them all, or wants to become a policeman or policewoman when he or she grows up, that person should write to the Police Department of New York City, if he lives in that city.

The police departments of most of the cities and towns all over the United States are set up in much the same way as the New York Police Department. Anyone who does not live in New York should write to his own police department.

This is the complete list of the membership of the Police Department of New York City.

The whole Police Department of the city is very much like an army — not an army to make war, but an army to make peace and to protect the people of the city.

The enemies of this peaceful police army are of course the criminals who will not obey the laws, and the enemies are the accidents and other unpleasant things, like storms, fires, explosions, and disasters, that might hurt the people this army protects.

But the man who governs and directs this peaceful army is usually not a trained policeman.

He is the Police Commissioner. He is appointed by the Mayor of the city because he has the experience and ability to govern and direct a big organization such as the Police Department.

The Police Commissioner appoints seven Deputy Commissioners. They help him govern the Police Department.

The Chief Inspector is the commanding officer of the whole Police Department. He is appointed by the Police Commissioner because of the good work he has done as a policeman and as a higher officer in the Police Department.

The Chief of Staff is the chief assistant to the Chief Inspector.

The Chief of Detectives is the head of the Detective Division.

There are a number of Deputy Chief Inspectors, and there are Inspectors and Deputy Inspectors.

The next in command are the Captains, then the Lieutenants, then the Sergeants. Then follow Patrolmen (First Grade Detectives), Patrolmen (Second Grade Detectives), Patrolmen (Third Grade Detectives), then Patrolmen.

All the officers and policemen are appointed by the Police Commissioner after they have taken examinations and after they have proved that they know their work and are brave and that they deserve to be promoted.

Now and then many policemen, policewomen, and officers are given medals for their excellent work and their courage. They deserve their medals. They are one of the finest and bravest groups of men and women in the world.

Index